**ROCKFORD PUBLIC LIBRARY**

Rockford, Illinois

www.rockfordpubliclibrary.org

815-965-9511

# F-16 FIGHTING FALCONS

## BY DENNY VON FINN

**EPIC**

BELLWETHER MEDIA · MINNEAPOLIS, MN

# EPIC

**EPIC BOOKS** are no ordinary books. They burst with intense action, high-speed heroics, and shadows of the unknown. Are you ready for an Epic adventure?

Range    50    100

THREAT DETECTED

This edition first published in 2013 by Bellwether Media, Inc.

No part of this publication may be reproduced in whole or in part without written permission of the publisher. For information regarding permission, write to Bellwether Media, Inc., Attention: Permissions Department, 5357 Penn Avenue South, Minneapolis, MN 55419.

Library of Congress Cataloging-in-Publication Data

Von Finn, Denny.
F-16 Fighting Falcons / by Denny Von Finn.
   p. cm. – (Epic: military vehicles)
Includes bibliographical references and index.
Summary: "Engaging images accompany information about F-16 Fighting Falcons. The combination of high-interest subject matter and light text is intended for students in grades 2 through 7"–Provided by publisher.
Audience: Grades 2-7.
ISBN 978-1-60014-884-2 (hbk. : alk. paper)
1. F-16 (Jet fighter plane)–Juvenile literature. I. Title.
UG1242.F5V653 2013
623.74'64–dc23                    2012033443

Printed in the United States of America, North Mankato, MN.

The photographs in this book are reproduced through the courtesy of the United States Department of Defense. A special thanks to Ted Carlson/Fotodynamics for contributing the cover photo and the photos on pp. 4-5, 10, 11, 12-13, 16, 17, 18, 18-19, 20-21.

# TABLE OF CONTENTS

# F-16 FIGHTING FALCONS

Range

THREAT DETECTED

RESCUE

Four pilots dash across an **airfield**. Within seconds they are roaring across the sky in their F-16 Fighting Falcons.

0      50      100

THREAT DETECTED

AK

AF
BG 293

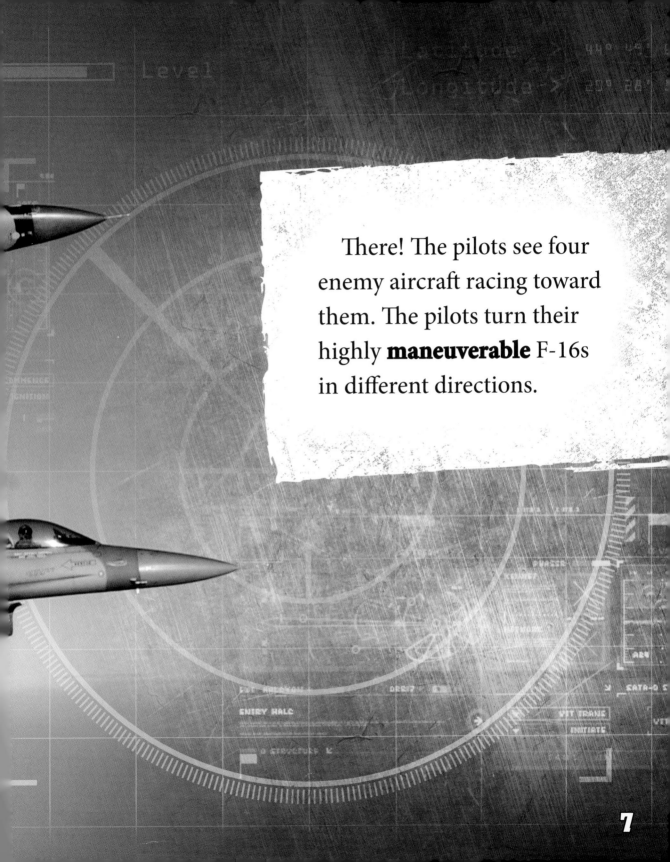

There! The pilots see four enemy aircraft racing toward them. The pilots turn their highly **maneuverable** F-16s in different directions.

The F-16s reappear behind the enemy fighters. The pilots fire their **missiles**. Balls of fire fill the sky. **Mission** accomplished!

Level

SW

7

# CREW, PARTS, AND WEAPONS

HUD

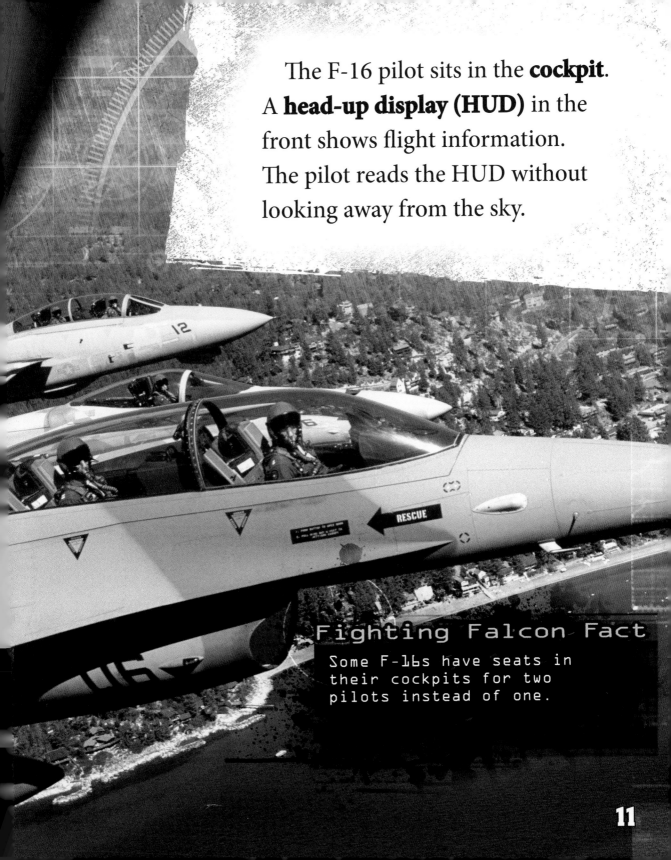

The F-16 pilot sits in the **cockpit**. A **head-up display (HUD)** in the front shows flight information. The pilot reads the HUD without looking away from the sky.

Fighting Falcon Fact

Some F-16s have seats in their cockpits for two pilots instead of one.

The F-16 has a powerful jet engine. It can fly up to 1,500 miles (2,414 kilometers) per hour. That is twice the speed of sound!

JET ENGINE

F-16 FLYING FASTER THAN
THE SPEED OF SOUND

Quick turns at high speeds cause extreme **g-forces**. The F-16 **airframe** is built to handle these g-forces.

Fighting Falcon Fact

The F-16 airframe carries bombs, missiles, and extra fuel tanks.

# VEHICLE BREAKDOWN: F-16 FIGHTING FALCON

| | |
|---|---|
| **Used By:** | U.S. Air Force |
| | U.S. Navy |
| **Entered Service:** | 1979 |
| **Length:** | 49.4 feet (15.1 meters) |
| **Height:** | 16 feet (4.9 meters) |
| **Wingspan:** | 32.7 feet (10 meters) |
| **Maximum Takeoff Weight:** | 37,500 pounds (17,010 kilograms) |
| **Top Speed:** | 1,500 miles (2,414 kilometers) per hour |
| **Range:** | more than 2,000 miles (3,219 kilometers) |
| **Ceiling:** | more than 50,000 feet (15,240 meters) |
| **Crew:** | 1 or 2 |
| **Weapons:** | bombs, missiles, 20mm cannon |
| **Nickname:** | Viper |
| **Primary Missions:** | air-to-air combat, air-to-ground attack |

# F-16 MISSIONS

Latitude
Longitude

VT
158FW

16

The F-16 is a **multi-role** fighter. It attacks enemy planes in the sky. It also finds and destroys ground targets.

An F-16 can reach targets more than 500 miles (805 kilometers) away in darkness or bad weather. **Radar** helps F-16 pilots locate targets and **navigate**.

RADAR

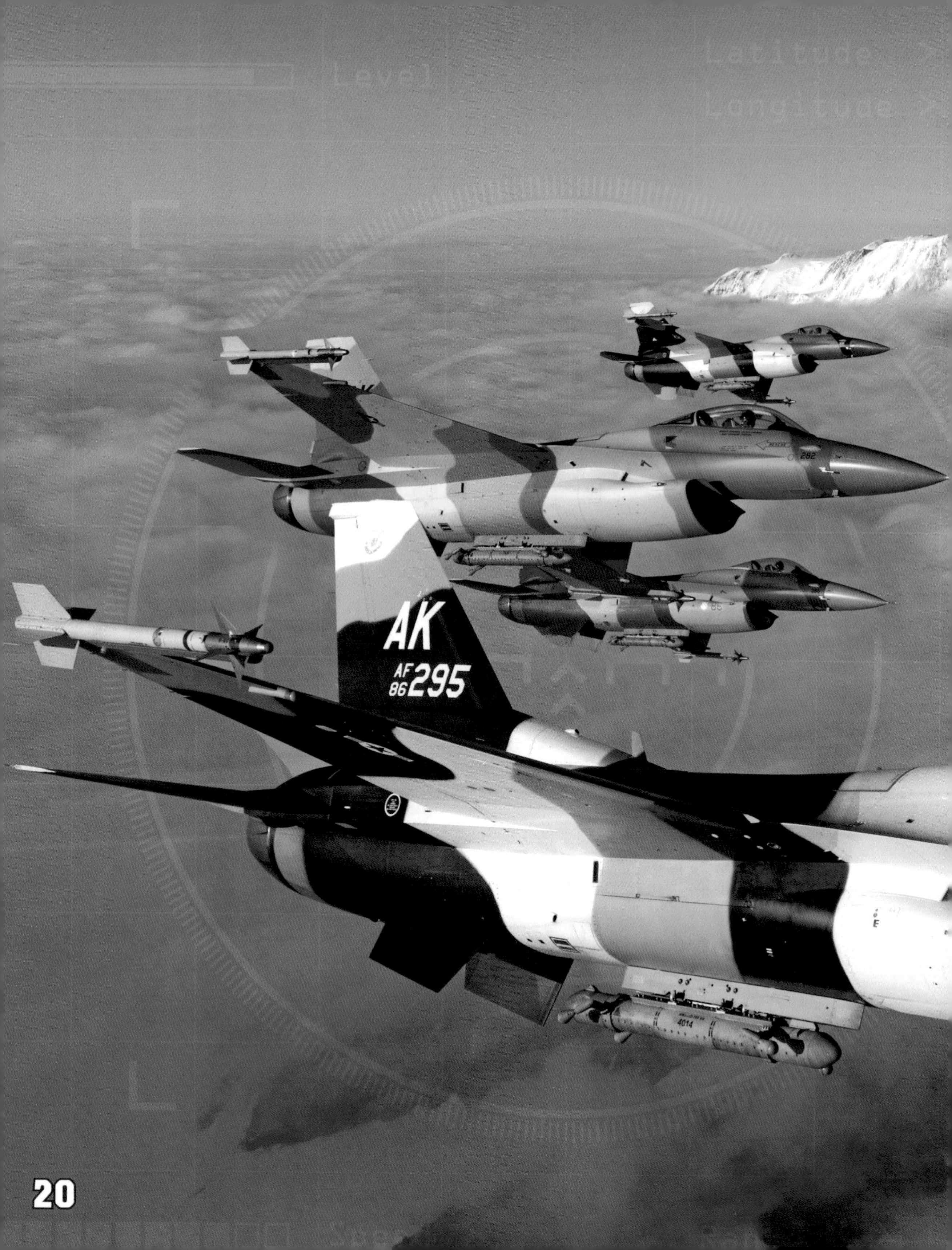
Level
Latitude >
Longitude >
AK
AF
86 295

F-16s flew many missions in the **Gulf War** and the **War on Terror**. They will continue to serve the United States for many years.

## Fighting Falcon Fact

More than 4,500 F-16s have been built. They are used in more than 20 countries.

RESCUE

295

# GLOSSARY

**airfield**—a place where aircraft can gather, take off, and land

**airframe**—the body and wings of an aircraft

**cockpit**—the area inside an aircraft where the pilot sits

**g-forces**—the pressures that high speeds and quick turns place on a pilot

**Gulf War**—a conflict from 1990 to 1991 in which 34 nations fought against Iraq; the war began after Iraq invaded the small country of Kuwait.

**head-up display (HUD)**—a clear glass screen that displays information in front of a pilot

**maneuverable**—able to change speed and direction very quickly

**missiles**—explosives that are guided to a target

**mission**—a military task

**multi-role**—able to perform more than one task

**navigate**—to guide an aircraft to its target and back

**radar**—a system that uses radio waves to locate targets

**War on Terror**—a war led by the United States to stop organized groups from performing acts of violence; the War on Terror began in 2001.

# TO LEARN MORE

## At the Library

Hamilton, John. *F-16 Fighting Falcon*. Minneapolis, Minn.:
ABDO Pub. Co., 2012.

Von Finn, Denny. *Jet Fighters*. Minneapolis, Minn.:
Bellwether Media, 2010.

Von Finn, Denny. *Supersonic Jets*. Minneapolis, Minn.:
Bellwether Media, 2010.

## On the Web

Learning more about F-16 Fighting Falcons
is as easy as 1, 2, 3.

1. Go to www.factsurfer.com.

2. Enter "F-16 Fighting Falcons" into the search box.

3. Click the "Surf" button and you will see a list
of related Web sites.

With factsurfer.com, finding more information
is just a click away.

# INDEX

THREAT DETECTED